In many ways, Berlin defies description. It has never been the prettiest or most polished European city, and yet it has easily enchanted so many – not just today, but in many generations past. When David Bowie moved to Berlin in the late 1970s to record what would be some of his most successful albums, he famously described it as "the greatest cultural extravaganza that one could imagine". All these years later, his words still ring true, to me as well as to the countless others who have fallen for this lively, spunky, iconoclast of a city.

Despite its tumultuous 20th-century history and the sweeping changes since the reunification of East and West Berlin, the capital has remained true to its unique character. Today's Berlin is just the right balance of things from the past and new trends, high culture and low. This is a place full of action, shot through with an independent spirit and a love of a good time, and it's so much fun to discover.

the hunt berlin writer

hilda hoy

Hilda Hoy is a journalist and writer who ended up in Berlin as a result of a very happy coincidence: after leaving a newspaper job in Prague, Berlin just happened to be a nearby place to take an extended holiday – one that has lasted nine years and counting. When not covering local dining and nightlife for *Where Berlin* magazine, she can be found tilling her allotment garden, scouring flea markets or exploring all corners of the city by bike, U-Bahn and on foot. She writes about the places she finds on her blog, thenwetakeberlin.de.

where to lay your weary head

Rest up, relax and recharge

DAS STUE HOTEL

DAS STUE HOTEL

Pure park-side luxury

Drakestrasse 1 (near Thomas-Dehler-Strasse; Tiergarten)
+49 30 311 7220 / das-stue.com

Double from €250

If the façade of Das Stue seems stately in appearance, that's because it is.
The 1930s building that was once the Royal Danish Embassy has been transformed
into one of Berlin's most well-appointed accommodations, with rain showers,
an HD Apple entertainment system and floor-to-ceiling windows. In line with the
building's legacy of international diplomacy, the hotel enlisted Spanish designers
to create its sleek, contemporary look, and the Michelin-starred Cinco restaurant
is led by Catalan chef Paco Pérez. There's art to admire around every corner,
and the location on the edge of Tiergarten Park means most rooms look onto
lush landscape or the neighboring zoo.

GORKI APARTMENTS

Home away from home

Weinbergsweg 25 (near Torstrasse; Mitte)
+49 30 4849 6480 / gorkiapartments.com

Double from €130

Settle in like a local with your very own designer abode. Gorki Apartments has converted a turn-of-the-century building into swanky holiday rentals, giving travelers the independence they crave, complete with the attentive service of a hotel. From cozy studios to luxe penthouses with private rooftop terraces, each apartment features modish yet homey design and upmarket features like claw-foot tubs. The area, just steps from Rosenthaler Platz station and plenty of restaurants and bars, couldn't be more convenient.

GORKI APARTMENTS

HONIGMOND HOTELS

HONIGMOND HOTELS

Secluded, old-fashioned romance

Tieckstrasse 11 (near Borsigstrasse; Mitte)
+49 30 284 4550 / honigmond.de

Double from € 129

No cookie-cutter décor here. Every room at the small, privately run Honigmond – the name means "honeymoon" – has a historic character all its own, with features like grand four-poster beds, gilded ceilings with ornate stucco, antique parquet floors and brocade wallpaper in royal shades of forest green and peacock blue. At the second site around the corner, rooms open out onto a private courtyard garden, creating a peaceful oasis in the heart of the city.

MICHELBERGER HOTEL

The life of the party

Warschauer Strasse 39-40 (near Tamara-Danz-Strasse; Friedrichshain)
+49 30 2977 8590 / michelbergerhotel.com

Double from €95

Looking for a fun hotel? This is it. The Michelberger has a youthful, irreverent vibe from head to toe, from the playful, funky treatments of the rooms and common spaces to the animated rocket ships that dance across its website. The flexible lodging concepts range from intimate, couples-friendly love nests to big suites that sleep six. The bar and all-organic restaurant are popular hangouts even among non-guests, and when the nightlife starts calling your name, Friedrichshain's raucous party district is practically on the front steps.

THE DUDE

Classic and crisp

Köpenicker Strasse 92 (at Neue Jakobstrasse; Mitte)
+49 30 411 988 177 / thedudeberlin.com

Double from €129

The Dude prides itself on being more like a private mansion than a hotel. Each of the rooms dotted throughout the historic building is kitted out with brightly colored walls and gold-accented furnishings that combine to look reminiscent of America's Jazz Age. The cigar lounge has an amply stocked humidor of Cubans that can be enjoyed while lazing on overstuffed leather couches, and its steakhouse, The Brooklyn, is famed for its delectable Black Angus cuts and whiskey selection. The owner himself, Alexander Schmidt-Vogel, is on hand to see through the hotel's commitment to personalized service.

WEINMEISTER HOTEL

Location, location, location

Weinmeisterstrasse 2 (near Rosenthaler Strasse; Mitte)
+49 30 755 6670 / the-weinmeister.com

Double from £ 95

Right in the middle of it all yet somewhat hidden behind an unassuming, graffiti-covered door, the Weinmeister has streamlined, minimal rooms and an address that can't be beat. All of Mitte's best shopping, dining, drinking and dancing are within short walking distance, but first you'll have to drag yourself away from your oversized, extra-comfy bed, one of the key features in every room. The hotel enlisted artists and musicians to design six different signature rooms, and there are also street art murals in the staircases and at the front entrance.

WEINMEISTER HOTEL

kreuzberg

Edgy, youthful and vibrant, Kreuzberg is the neighborhood that best sums up the spirit of modern-day Berlin. It's the first place I lived when I moved here in 2007, but I love Kreuzberg for more than sentimental reasons. Cool and laid-back, this area has it all: awesome restaurants, countless drinking joints both classy and hole-in-the-wall, animated street life and the pretty, willow-lined Landwehr Canal. It's also the original home of Berlin's sizeable Turkish community, making this one of the most multicultural parts of the city. In the '70s and '80s, it was ground zero for artists, students, squatters and punks; though it's now a desirable place for young families and yuppies, that legacy of alternative subcultures is still palpable in the enclave's graffitied streets. Spend a few days hanging out here and you'll understand the hype.

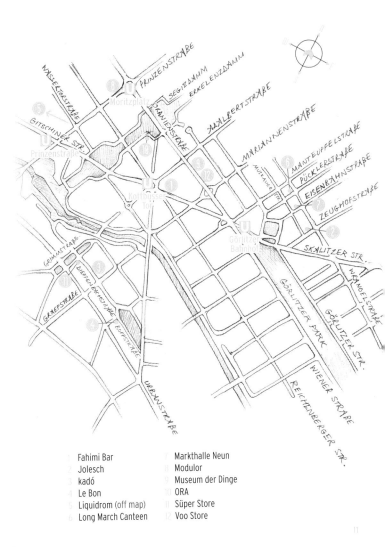

1   Fahimi Bar   7   Markthalle Neun
2   Jolesch   8   Modulor
3   kadó   9   Museum der Dinge
4   Le Bon   10 ORA
5   Liquidrom (off map)   11 Süper Store
6   Long March Canteen   12 Voo Store

FAHIMI BAR

Highballs by the highline

Skalitzer Strasse 133 (near Adalberstrasse) / **+49 30 6165 6003**
fahimibar.de / **Closed Monday**

On any given night, Kottbusser Tor is where the action is. This hectic junction is where transit lines – and groups of partygoers – meet, and from a second-floor perch at Fahimi Bar, you're primed to take it all in. Behind a grimy, graffiti- and sticker-covered entrance, and up a flight of stairs lies a stylish, minimal bar with concrete walls and big windows looking out onto the elevated U1 line. There's nothing like sipping a cocktail while yellow trains zip by at eye level to make you feel like you're at the very heart of the capital. For drinks, I recommend their signature Hazard Fashioned, which is rye, cognac, maple syrup and chocolate bitters.

JOLESCH

Elegant Austrian cuisine by the fire

Muskauer Strasse 1 (at Zeughofstrasse) / **+49 30 612 3581**
jolesch.de / **Open daily**

With marble tabletops, golden chandeliers and emerald-green walls,
Jolesch sports a stately, sophisticated look while still feeling like a snug
corner locale – the crackling fire might have something to do with that.
The classics section of the menu features hearty mainstays like goulash
and veal schnitzel – which, by the way, is among the finest in the city, and
I've tried many. Much as I'm loyal to that golden-crisp schnitzel, I'm happy
to report that everything I've tasted from the more progressive section
of the menu, which changes frequently to take advantage of what's in
season, has been equally delectable.

KADÓ

A candy shop for connoisseurs

Graefestrasse 20 (at Dieffenbachstrasse) / +49 30 6904 1638
kado.de / Closed Sunday and Monday

Black licorice is one of those things people either love or hate. I was once in the latter camp, but at some point the tables turned and now I can't get enough of the stuff — with its layers of complex, intense flavors, it's like candy for the discerning. Given the success of kadó, an old-timey confectionery that sells nothing but black licorice, I'm far from alone in my love for it. Sourced from around the globe, the vast amount of treats on offer ranges from intense Scandinavian and Dutch varieties to licorice chocolate from Iceland. It's scooped out of glass jars and sold by weight, so you can try as much variety as your taste buds can handle.

LE BON

Satisfying brunches and dinners

Boppstrasse 1 (at Schönleinstrasse) / **+49 30 6342 0794**
lebon-berlin.com / **Closed Monday**

Whether you call it breakfast or brunch, the first meal of the day is the best as far as I'm concerned. For special occasions or just to treat myself, hip, chill Le Bon is my go-to place. Served from early morning hours until late in the afternoon, the brekkie menu is a delectable smorgasbord of options that incorporates influences from owner Johanna's travels to cities that are crazy about the midday meal, like Melbourne and Tel Aviv. The eggs Benedict and the spicy shakshuka (poached eggs with tomatoes, chili peppers, onions and cumin) are enduringly favored, however, I'm a devotee of the granola pancakes with caramelized bananas. In the evenings, an equally scrumptious dinner menu takes over.

LIQUIDROM

Soak and sweat away stress

**Möckernstrasse 10 (at Hallesche Strasse) / +49 30 258 007 820
liquidrom-berlin.de / Open daily**

Germans are big believers in the health-giving benefits of a good sauna
session, and Liquidrom is an upscale, Zen-styled spa where you can sweat
it out. There are various options ranging from mild to gaspingly hot as well
as massage treatments on offer, but the star attraction is the big saltwater
flotation pool that shimmers under a dim, hushed dome. As you lie back
and float weightlessly, underwater speakers play soothing, trippy tunes
that are provided by live DJs on weekend nights. Take note: as per German
custom, swimsuits are verboten in the (mixed-gender) saunas. Hey, there's
no better way to get to know the locals, right?

LONG MARCH CANTEEN

Chinese fusion served dim sum-style

Wrangelstrasse 20 (at Pücklerstrasse) / +49 178 884 9599
longmarchcanteen.com / Open daily

Being half-Taiwanese myself, the food of that corner of the world naturally holds a special place in my greedy little heart. Long March Canteen puts a creative twist on the dim sum concept, wheeling small plates of delicacies from table to table on a metal cart – Hong Kong-style. From the billowing steam of the open kitchen emerge stacks of steamer baskets concealing juicy dumplings, made either the conventional way with pork and ginger or with funky fillings like scallops and sweet potato. How about some jellyfish carpaccio, grilled baby squid or glazed sparerib bonbons? Can't make up your mind? You'll just have to try it all.

MARKTHALLE NEUN

Foodie central

Eisenbahnstrasse 42-43 (near Wrangelstrasse) / **+49 30 6107 3473**
markthalleneun.de / **Closed Sunday**

One of the city's only 19th-century market halls to survive, Markthalle Neun has been at the center of Kreuzberg's culinary revival in recent years. Under the hall's soaring, vaulted roof, a farmers market takes place three days a week and food-loving entrepreneurs have set up permanent bases inside as well, making and selling things like microbrewed India pale ale, artisanal sourdough loaves, smoked fish and Tennessee-style barbecued ribs that are finger-licking good. Most favored of all is the weekly Street Food Thursday event, which sees food stands cramming the hall, hawking scrumptious, freshly made delicacies from around the globe.

MODULOR

Get crafty

Prinzenstrasse 85 (at Moritzplatz) / **+49 30 690 360**
modulor.de / **Closed Sunday**

Nothing leaves me more inspired than a visit to Modulor. This huge,
multi-leveled purveyor of art and design supplies is where architects,
artists and other creative professionals stock up on tools of the trade, but it
also has plenty of goods that appeal to wannabes like me. From the fabric,
crafting wares and gift wrap to the notebooks, model-building materials and
every stationery item imaginable, Modulor can inspire anyone to get their
hands dirty and make stuff. Need a sheet of colored acrylic laser-cut into the
form of your choosing? Yup, Modulor can do that.

MUSEUM DER DINGE

The art of the everyday

Oranienstrasse 25 (near Adalbertstrasse) / **+49 30 9210 6311**
museumderdinge.de / **Closed Tuesday and Wednesday**

The stuff on exhibit at the Museum der Dinge, which translates to
Museum of Things, are daily objects in all their plain glory, elevated from
mundane to marvelous simply by being showcased in glass vitrines.
From rubber duckies to soap packets, salt and pepper shakers to wind-
up toys, the thousands of items in the collection are eclectically yet
cleverly organized by material, color, era or usage. The result is a quirky,
lighthearted overview of design trends as well as a visualization of life
in Germany over the past century, told not by its inhabitants but by the
weird, beautiful and sometimes utterly tasteless things they left behind.

ORA

From pharmacy to phenomenal café

Oranienplatz 14 (at Erkelenzdamm) / No phone
facebook.com/oraberlin / Open daily

Berlin is a city very much in touch with its history. Sometimes that can be painful, but in the case of ORA, it's just splendid. Not long ago, this charming piece of corner retail space was a chemist's, where the gray-haired geriatrics of the neighborhood picked up their prescriptions. When converting the space into a café, restaurant and bar rolled into one, the makers of ORA wisely kept the pharmacy's 19th-century wooden cabinets and shelves, which are still lined with antique apothecary jars. The ambiance is equally lovely for coffee and a cinnamon bun in the morning, or late at night for a cocktail. Their drinks change seasonally and a particularly memorable one was the Rhubarb Fizz with rhubarb-infused gin, mandarin schnapps, soda and lemon.

SÜPER STORE

All things delightful

**Dieffenbachstrasse 12 (near Grimmstrasse) / +49 30 9832 7944
sueper-store.de / Closed Sunday and Monday**

Epitomizing the virtues of quality over quantity, the selection at Süper Store may be small, but it is simply exquisite. Every item in the inventory – from jewelry and glassware to lamps, art prints and home décor – has been carefully selected, either because it exemplifies artisanal, handmade quality or it tells a story of timeless design. One purchase I treasure is a pair of filigree scissors shaped like a stork, which German midwives in the 1800s used to cut umbilical cords. I've also got my eye on the shop's delicate Modernist mobiles from the legendary Flensted company in Denmark, and the clear globe paperweights that each contain a gorgeous dandelion puff.

VOO STORE

Clothes for hip kids

Oranienstrasse 24 (near Adalbertstrasse) / +49 30 695 797 2710
vooberlin.com / Closed Sunday

Voo Store is like that one friend you can always count on to look flawlessly
cool no matter what they wear. Secreted away in a back courtyard, this
spacious venue stocks an impeccably curated mix of low-key hipster
threads for both men and women, ranging from super-fashionable brands
like A.P.C. and Acne Studios to niche, cult labels from our smartly dressed
Scandinavian neighbors, such as Soulland, Wood Wood and Henrik Vibskov.
In addition to clothing, it also carries perfumes, accessories, footwear and
books. And the icing on the cake? The in-house café makes a really stellar
cup of coffee.

turkish berlin

Sights, smells and tastes of a multicultural city

Were it not for the influence of its hundreds of thousands of Turkish residents, Berlin would be a much less interesting place. These immigrants are the largest non-European minority here, and they have left a distinct mark on Kreuzberg in particular. Rub shoulders with them every Tuesday and Friday at the **Turkish Market**, a bustling outdoor scene next to the Landwehr Canal. One of the biggest open-air markets in the city, this is where Turkish housewives and bargain-hunting folks stock up on fresh produce, flatbread, olives, cheese and other essentials.

Next stop on the tour of Turkey's delectable cuisine should be **Doyum Restaurant**, a hole-in-the-wall kebab joint tucked behind the Kottbusser Tor intersection. The hand-painted blue tiles on the walls make for a bit of a juxtaposition against the fluorescent lights flickering overhead, but the scores of Turkish families and taxi drivers eating here at all hours are a testament to the tasty grub. The unrivaled dish in the house is the Adana kebab, spicy ground lamb that's charcoal-grilled on a skewer, then served with rich tomato sauce and dollops of yogurt.

CONFISERIE ORIENTALE

To dine in a somewhat classier setting, on the other side of Kottbusser Tor is **Hasir**, a mainstay on the local scene since the early 1980s. Urban legend has it that the owner invented the döner kebab, the by-now ubiquitous street food sandwich. The customers that pack Hasir aren't here for the döner, however, but for the grilled meat and wealth of meze appetizers, feasting amidst framed photos of all the celebrities who have eaten here over the decades.

Every restaurant will have a tray of syrupy baklava at the ready, but to try a special kind of confection, Mitte's **Confiserie Orientale** is the place. Sweets boutique and café rolled into one, the confiserie specializes in classic marzipan and pastel-colored lokum, aka Turkish delight, which is made by hand using old-fashioned recipes. Flavored with rose, pomegranate and cardamom with pistachios and hazelnuts for added crunch, the delights pair perfectly with a cuppa.

For some pampering, Kreuzberg's **Hamam** is a traditional-style steam bath with treatments like thorough scrub downs with a kese (exfoliating) mitt and sabunlama (Oriental soaping) massages, as well as facials and hair removal with sugar syrup. After you emerge fresh, pink and scoured clean, there's tea waiting in the lounge area. Sorry, guys – this hamam has a women-only policy.

CONFISERIE ORIENTALE

HOTEL RESTAURANT

HAMAM

HASIR

TURKISH MARKET

TURKISH MARKET

mitte

Chock-full of shopping, galleries, museums, nightlife and dining to suit every taste, Mitte is the capital's polished, bustling center. Its name – which means "middle" in German – is technically a misnomer: Mitte is actually toward the east side of the city. Still, if I had to name one area as downtown, this would be it. When the Berlin Wall came down, Mitte (which belonged to East Germany) was in pretty rough shape, but over the last 15 years, it's gotten a spiffy and modern makeover. Friedrichstrasse and Alexanderplatz are now humming commercial districts, though the finest boutiques are clustered around Weinmeisterstrasse and Torstrasse, along with more restaurants and cafés than any reasonable person could ever hope to try.

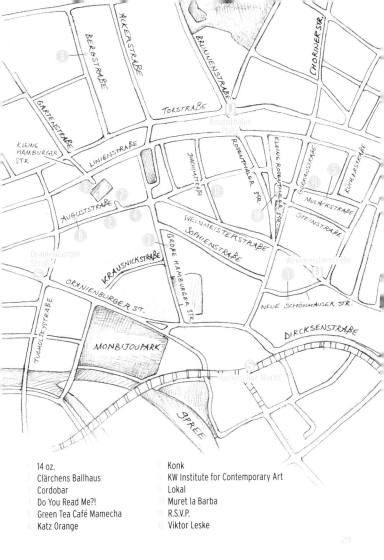

1	14 oz.
2	Clärchens Ballhaus
3	Cordobar
4	Do You Read Me?!
5	Green Tea Café Mamecha
6	Katz Orange
7	Konk
8	KW Institute for Contemporary Art
9	Lokal
10	Muret la Barba
11	R.S.V.P.
12	Viktor Leske

14 oz.

For fashionable gents

Neue Schönhauser Strasse 13 (near Rosenthaler Strasse)
+49 30 2804 0514 / 14oz.com / Closed Sunday

Many boutiques and labels out there focus on women's wear, but 14 oz. turns that formula around. Nearly the entire store is dedicated to looks for the fashion-forward gentleman, relegating the women's stuff to a few tables in the back. The selection is comprised of basic, high-quality wardrobe staples that every dapper man should own, like soft undershirts, rugged brogues and expertly crafted boots, iconic Baracuta G9 jackets made famous by Britain's mods and punks, classic Mackintosh raincoats and Japanese selvedge denim. Listen up, boys – these are looks that will likely meet your partner's approval.

CLÄRCHENS BALLHAUS

Swingin' the night away

Auguststrasse 24 (near Grosse Hamburger Strasse)
+49 30 282 9295 | ballhaus.de | Open daily

In the heart of a neighborhood that has modernized at a breathtaking pace in recent years, the centenarian Clärchens stands as a proud testament that old age can be cool. The dance hall opened in 1913 and has been a hot spot ever since, changing its appearance little over the years. There's dancing every night, from swing to tango to cha cha, including lessons to give novices a boost. On weekends, the soundtrack shifts toward pop hits and revelers of all ages pack the floor. I don't come here to dance, but I certainly enjoy the people-watching and classic ambiance. There's also food served until late and a beer garden out front during the summer.

CORDOBAR

Calling all wine lovers

Grosse Hamburger Strasse 32 (near Krausnickstrasse)
+49 30 2758 1215 / cordobar.net / **Closed Sunday and Monday**

Germany is better known around the world for its beers rather than its vino, but an evening at Cordobar is enough to change anybody's mind about that. Most labels in the massive inventory – nearly 1,000 bottles strong – come from Germany or Austria, including rarities that will send the oenophile's heart aflutter. Even for amateurs like me, there's plenty to celebrate. The changing menu of inventive, European-Asian fusion bar snacks includes things like succulent ribs and crispy pork skin, or the popular blood sausage pizza with beets and wasabi. Order a few to share, or get a bunch and call it dinner.

DO YOU READ ME?!

'Zines galore

Auguststrasse 28 (near Grosse Hamburger Strasse)
+49 30 6954 9695 / doyoureadme.de   Closed Sunday

Print newspapers may be in the throes of a slow and painful decline, but magazines are alive and thriving thanks to the influx of inspired, niche publications that keep hitting the market. Do You Read Me?! is the capital's leading periodical source, stocking popular lifestyle tomes like *Kinfolk* and *Cereal*, homegrown indie publications like *Berlin Quarterly*, eye-catching photography and fashion digests plus literary journals from around the world. My weakness is food magazines, so I make sure to stop by whenever there's a new issue of *Lucky Peach*.

GREEN TEA CAFÉ MAMECHA

Japanese tea and treats

Mulackstrasse 33 (near Rückerstrasse) / **+49 30 2888 4264**
mamecha.com / **Closed Sunday**

On a side street smack-dab in the middle of Mitte's trendiest shopping area, Mamecha is a peaceful and subdued respite that feels like a slice of Tokyo, serving teas, sweets and light meals. When I need a lift, I order a vibrantly green matcha latte – maybe with a slice of matcha cheesecake if I'm going all out. For a mellower break, the toasty hojicha hits the spot. Thanks to the self-serve hot water refills, you can reinfuse the leaves in the cute side-handled teapot as often as you like and linger long into the afternoon.

KATZ ORANGE

Homey, high-end food

Bergstrasse 22 (near Invalidenstrasse) | + 49 30 983 208 430
katzorange.com / Open daily

Tucked away in the courtyard of a one-time brewery, Katz Orange is
pleasing to look at inside and out. There's a relaxed vibe to both the
menu and the boho-chic interior, featuring exposed brick and lots of
throw pillows in folksy fabrics. Top-quality regional ingredients and
Slow Food principles have a major influence, like with the house
specialty: Duroc pork roasted for 12 hours until unbelievably tender.
Just try and resist the French fries crisped in luscious goose fat, and the
amazing cocktails — they make a great Negroni and an Old Fashioned
with cocoa bean-infused bourbon. I dare you.

KONK

Homegrown fashion

Kleine Hamburger Strasse 15 (near Auguststrasse)
+49 30 2809 7839 / **konk-berlin.de** / **Closed Sunday**

We've all been schooled by now on the virtues of eating locally, and Konk believes that applies to shopping, too. The impeccably curated boutique focuses exclusively on Berlin-based designers making everything from clothing to accessories to jewelry. Depending on the time of year, the rotating collection might include flowing summer dresses by Tim Labenda, tunics in wildly colorful prints by Anntian, sleek and sophisticated basics by Isabell de Hillerin or Nina Kastens' gold rings and bangles shaped like thorny brambles. I've always believed there's no better souvenir than the one you can wear.

KW INSTITUTE FOR CONTEMPORARY ART

Cutting-edge art

Auguststrasse 69 (near Tucholskystrasse) / +49 30 243 4590
kw-berlin.de / Closed Tuesday

Right in the middle of Mitte's most important gallery strip, the Kunst-Werke
– casually referred to by everyone as the KW – is the city's preeminent
institution for modern art. There are multiple exhibition spaces in the
back patio, but pieces are everywhere, even before you enter. The jagged
sidewalk out front is the work of Brazilian artist Renata Lucas, who rotated
the pavement exactly 7.5 degrees clockwise. Pay close attention to spot
installations on walls, façades and signposts, too. The exhibition openings,
film screenings, artist talks and performances here are always the best
places to mingle with the hippest artsy crowd.

LOKAL

For stylish locavores

Linienstrasse 160 (at Kleine Hamburger Strasse)
+49 30 2844 9500 / lokal-berlin.blogspot.de / **Open daily**

With pure white walls and rustic tables hewn from impressive hunks
of wood, the look at Lokal is part farmhouse, part architecture magazine
feature. As the name suggests, the focus is on seasonal produce, and the
menu changes weekly to take advantage of whatever's fresh – I fondly
remember a delightful blueberry spelt risotto I had last summer. The limits
of the North German climate demand creativity, so you may well discover
a new ingredient or two – things like purslane, chervil root and rose hip.
During hunting season, look for game on the menu: boar tongue or
venison tartare, anyone?

MURET LA BARBA

A taste of Italy

Rosenthaler Strasse 61 (near Steinstrasse) / +49 30 2809 7212
muretlabarba.de / Open daily

Four red letters on the exterior spelling out "wein" are the only sign
you're in the right place. Muret la Barba keeps outward appearances
simple, but the food and wine speak volumes. Lining the walls are
bottles of Italian vino sourced from Tuscany to Sicily and everywhere
in between. Perch on a stool in the front bar to nibble antipasti such as
oktopus-kartoffelsalat (octopus with potato, celery and capers) and sip
full-bodied Chianti, or snag a table in the back to feast on lunch and
dinner specials. A devoted carb addict, I always go for the homemade
pasta, whether delicate ravioli stuffed with whatever is in season or
tagliatelle with hearty ragù.

R.S.V.P.

Good old pen and paper

Mulackstrasse 14 (near Gormannstrasse) / **+49 30 2809 4644**
rsvp-berlin.de / **Closed Sunday**

So what if it's the digital age? Stationery fanatics like me know that no computer screen or keyboard will ever match the analog beauty of creamy, gorgeous letterhead and an exquisite writing implement. With its fine curation of notebooks, writing supplies and gift wrap, R.S.V.P. is a pretty slice of stationery heaven. There are brass pencil sharpeners from Germany, gold-plated scissors and letter openers from Italy, mechanical pencils from the Czech Republic and pens from Japan. Sweet greeting cards will have you believing in the power of snail mail all over again.

VIKTOR LESKE

The hottest tresses

Joachimstrasse 8 (near Auguststrasse) / +49 30 2790 8487
viktorleske.net / Closed Sunday and Monday

To fit in amongst this neighborhood's many hipsters, you'll want to have your look on point. An all-black outfit and a disaffected pout are musts, but nothing completes the picture like a sharp haircut. Book an appointment with Viktor himself to experience his trademark technique, using an electric clipper instead of scissors to buzz manes into perfect submission. With its striking industrial interior and dark techno beats on the stereo, getting a cut or color here feels like spending a few hours at the club. I never fail to leave with a smile on my face and a spring in my step, not to mention a fantastic new 'do.

berlin by bike

Cruise and explore on two wheels

FAT TIRE TOURS

From the very first glance, it's clear that Berlin and biking are a perfect match. Everywhere you go, you'll see cyclists zipping along the streets, taking advantage of the city's flat terrain and extensive network of bike paths. Getting around on two wheels is not only fun and efficient, it's also one of the best ways to explore – nothing beats being right in the thick of street life.

The easiest way to jump into the cycling fray is to join one of the **Fat Tire Tours**. With bicycle and guide provided, all you need to do is pedal along at a leisurely pace and enjoy the sights. Options range from a general city overview to specialized, history-themed tours, and even a food tour.

Once you're ready to venture out on your own, you'll need to secure a set of wheels. There are plentiful bike rentals all over, but to hit the road in style, **Zweitrad** is the place to go. The shop specializes in classic and very handsome Dutch models for rent (and for sale), free from the ads that most rental places slap on their cycles.

One of my favorite rides is to Treptower Park along Puschkinallee, a boulevard shaded by rows of towering plane trees. The destination is the park's **Soviet War Memorial**, a massive, jaw-dropping monument to the Soviet soldiers who died on our soil during WWII. When heading back, loop westward to ride

along the Mauerweg trail, along Kiefholzstrasse and Heidelberger Strasse. This route follows the former path of the Berlin Wall, and along the way are memorials and placards telling stories of life in the divided city.

When you've had enough of inner-city cycling and could use a bit more space to cruise, **Sanssouci Park** in Potsdam should be on the agenda. A 30-minute train ride southwest of the city center, this sprawling park dotted with splendid palaces and landscaped gardens was once the playground of the Prussian royal family. Given the park's sheer size, a bike is helpful for discovering all the pretty corners. Bring one on the train, or rent one upon arrival at Potsdam station.

To get even further immersed in nature, take a cycling outing to **Moorlake**, an idyllic forest tavern on the edge of the city. The round-trip ride from the Wannsee S-Bahn station is about 11 km (7 miles), winding through oak and beech forest before threading along the shore of the Havel River. Once you arrive at Moorlake, a hot meal and cold beer await.

neukölln

Neukölln lies just south of Kreuzberg, and the two are close cousins – the places where the neighborhoods bleed into one another have been nicknamed Kreuzkölln. Indeed, Neukölln and Kreuzberg are similar: loud, lively, multicultural and hip. The Neukölln hype has only really taken off more recently, and it's less gentrified, rougher around the edges and still constantly changing. It's also been my home for the last six years, and I have no intention of ever leaving. What draws many people here are the plentiful drinking joints and cafés where artsy crowds love to gather. Hermannplatz is something of a community hub. From here, you can head down Sonnenallee or toward the canal for the busy bar district around Reuterstrasse and Weserstrasse, or head uphill on Hermannstrasse, where the enormous Tempelhofer Feld, a former airport turned public space, sits.

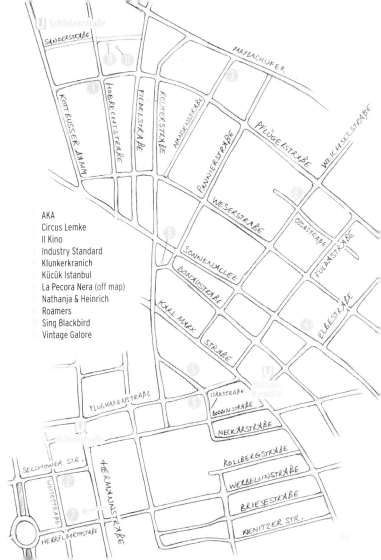

AKA
Circus Lemke
Il Kino
Industry Standard
Klunkerkranich
Kücük Istanbul
La Pecora Nera (off map)
Nathanja & Heinrich
Roamers
Sing Blackbird
Vintage Galore

AKA

Stunning body art

**Pflügerstrasse 6 (near Hobrechtstrasse) / +49 30 5564 2195
akaberlin.com / Closed Sunday and Monday**

A new tattoo would be the ultimate Berlin memento, I say. For something truly exceptional, AKA is where you should be. Seeing itself not as a conventional studio but as a hybrid art venue, AKA hosts regular exhibitions in their shop and works with incredibly talented inkers from a variety of creative backgrounds, which includes a roster of resident experts as well as visiting tattooists from around the world. These artists work in a wide range of styles – from minimalist to hyper-realistic – to create lifelong works of beauty on every client's skin.

CIRCUS LEMKE

Neighborhood bar

Selchower Strasse 31 (near Weisestrasse) / No phone
facebook.com/circuslemke / Open daily

The well-trodden drinking district of Neukölln is located down
around Hermannplatz and the canal, but up on the hill, revolving near
Schillerpromenade, is a more low-key enclave with a nightlife scene.
This is the hood I call home, and Circus Lemke is my most-loved local
watering hole. The one-room outfit is run by a group of friends who
created a warm, welcoming, good-looking establishment for a classic
cocktail or just a beer. It's the kind of place that is simply cool without
trying to be, with none of the so-hip-it-hurts attitude that today's
Neukölln can go overboard with.

IL KINO

Picturehouse and bar

Nansenstrasse 22 (near Maybachufer) / **+49 1577 681 1535**
ilkino.de / **Open daily**

Forget popcorn and candy. At this tiny cinema, you can sip a glass of
Montepulciano d'Abruzzo and snack on some plump Sicilian olives as
you watch a movie. With barely 40 seats, this theater is an intimate
venue featuring a thoughtful selection of films from around the world,
ranging from blockbusters to indies. Even if the program of the day
doesn't strike your fancy, you can still hang out – the front two rooms,
decorated with old movie posters, houses a welcoming Italian-style bistro
with panini, antipasti and a variety of wines. Movies and vino: what a
genius combination.

INDUSTRY STANDARD

Raising the bar on local dining

Sonnenallee 83 (near Elbestrasse) / **+49 30 6272 7732**
industry-standard.de / **Closed Monday and Tuesday**

I would sum up Industry Standard with one word: bold. Neukölln has
very few dining options of this price category — the most in-demand
food in this hood is probably a €3 Lebanese shawarma — and the busy,
bustling street it calls home is a bit incongruous with haute cuisine.
But the team behind this concept has the guts and gusto to pull it off
and quickly became the talk of the town after opening in early 2015.
The French-Mediterranean menu is refreshed regularly, but the legendary
beef tartare and delectable roasted bone marrow are staples. Expect lots
of pared-down, striking plates with a penchant for atypical produce and
meats, from ox tongue to reindeer.

KLUNKERKRANICH

Rooftop utopia

Neukölln Arcaden, Karl-Marx-Strasse 66 (at Flughafenstrasse)
No phone / klunkerkranich.de / Open daily

It's easy to love Klunkerkranich for its soaring panoramic views —
a rarity in a metropolis with so few high-rises. But what I really love
about Klunkerkranich is the DIY spirit it exemplifies, which is something
very unique to Berlin. Bar, club, event space and community garden all
rolled into one, Klunkerkranich is a makeshift village built by hand out
of recycled materials on the roof of a mall parking lot, a one-of-a-kind
spot to sunbathe in the summer (or get comfortable in a heated yurt
in the winter). Wiggle your toes in the sandbox, get your hands dirty
volunteering in the garden, have a drink in the glow of a golden sunset
and then dance to live music or DJs late into the night.

KÜÇÜK ISTANBUL

Old-school grooming for modern gents

Flughafenstrasse 15 (near Isarstrasse) / **+49 30 8101 9495**
kücükistanbul.de / **Open daily**

I don't have a beard myself – for obvious reasons – but if I did, this is
definitely where I'd come for the all-important upkeep. Styled like an
old-fashioned barbershop, with a grandfather clock ticking in the corner
and vinyl records playing on a gramophone, Küçük Istanbul is run by two
suspenders-wearing brothers who are passionate about the time-honored
craft of the barber. Their specialty is classic haircuts from the 1940s and
1950s, and the perfect shave comes courtesy of steaming-hot towels
and a straight razor. There might even be a quick massage thrown in.
Because deep down, men like a little pampering, too.

LA PECORA NERA

Scrumptious Venetian fare

Herrfurthplatz 6 (near Herrfurthstrasse) / **+49 30 6883 2676**
pecoraberlin.de / **Closed Monday**

Italian food may be one of the most popular cuisines around, but this
laid-back osteria sets itself well apart from the masses with a focus on the
lesser-known eats from the northern Veneto region. Polenta is big up there,
and La Pecora Nera serves theirs grilled, smothered in melted cheese then
topped with mushrooms or salsiccia sausage – simple, delectable comfort
food. This is one of my choice restaurants, mainly because I'm addicted to
their bigoli: fat, chewy, tube-shaped pasta noodles topped with a heap of
rich duck and parmesan ragù – mamma mia. Every Friday, the chef whips
up a few seafood specials using the catch of the day.

NATHANJA & HEINRICH

A proper night out

Weichselstrasse 44 (at Ossastrasse) / **no phone**
nathanja-heinrich.de / **Open daily**

Raw, unfinished walls – check. Mismatched vintage furniture – check. Extra-smoky atmosphere – check. Nathanja & Heinrich is the quintessential Neukölln drinking joint in more ways than one. Once a shop selling custom sports trophies (look above the bar and you might spot an old one), this corner space just off the area's busiest nightlife strip – that would be Weserstrasse – has high ceilings and huge windows opening onto the sidewalk. Nonetheless, things feel pretty snug every night of the week, when the venue teems with the hood's hipster populace. Pots of fresh herbs line the counter for making the house special, the Gin Basil Smash.

ROAMERS

Homey, Instagram-worthy brunch

Pannierstrasse 64 (at Donaustrasse) / No phone
roamersberlin.tumblr.com / Closed Monday

Everything about this café is just pretty as a picture: the hanging macramé planters overflowing with greenery, the rustic wooden furnishings and bartop, the adorable cactus arrangements, right down to the lush, artfully garnished plates. I'd describe the look as "bucolic barn meets Baja California". Whatever you want to call it, it works, and the eatery is one of the most beloved brunch spots in Neukölln. The giant Bloody Marys topped with crispy bacon and a whole pickle might have something to do with that. Get yours with a Lonesome Cowboy breakfast sandwich, featuring avocado, jalapeños and a perfectly fried egg.

SING BLACKBIRD

Secondhand shopping with a coffee break

Sanderstrasse 11 (near Hobrechtstrasse) / **+49 30 5484 5051**
singblackbird.tumblr.com / **Open daily**

While other parts of the German capital tend to be more brand conscious –
I'm looking at you, Mitte the typical outfit in this hood is definitely more
of a vintage mishmash. Sing Blackbird always has a solid selection of gently
used clothes, bags, sunglasses, jewelry and even shoes for shoppers to
pore over. Though there's a pretty good mix of styles, I find the general look
leans toward the nerdy-cool '80s and '90s aesthetic that's back in fashion
these days. The tiny café in the front room has java, cakes and cold-pressed
juice for a pre- or post-shopping pick-me-up.

VINTAGE GALORE

Marvelous home furnishings and threads

Sanderstrasse 12 (near Hobrechtstrasse) / +49 30 6396 3338
vintagegalore.de / Closed Sunday

Thanks to *Mad Men*, a whole generation of TV viewers has been left with an enduring obsession with 1950s and 1960s elegance and glam — myself included. Vintage Galore is where I go to stoke fantasies about the mid-century modern home of my dreams. The shop packs an impressive curation of fetching antique specimens into just two rooms, featuring pieces that hail primarily from Scandinavia. Besides teak dining sets, sofas, shelves and sideboards in mint condition, there are also stunning lamps, one-of-a-kind vases and ceramics, plus a tidy assortment of smart throwback fashion.

german cuisine, reinvented

Progressive updates on classic dishes

EINS44
Elbestrasse 28–29 (near Weserstrasse; Neukölln)
+49 30 6298 1212, eins44.com
closed Sunday and Monday

FÖLLEREI
Weichselstrasse 30 (near Oswaldstrasse; Neukölln)
+49 30 6093 0276, foellerei.de, open daily

HERZ & NIERE
Fichtestrasse 31 (near Urbanstrasse; Kreuzberg)
+49 30 6900 1522, herzundniere.berlin
closed Monday

MARTHA'S
Grunewaldstrasse 81 (near Gleditschstrasse;
Schöneberg), +49 30 7800 6665, marthas.berlin
open daily

VOLT
Paul-Lincke-Ufer 21 (near Ohlauer Strasse;
Kreuzberg), +49 30 338 402 320, restaurant-volt.de
closed Sunday and Monday

Before moving to Berlin, I never thought much of German cuisine – sausages? sauerkraut? – but living and eating here has broadened my culinary horizons. In recent years, a new generation of chefs and restaurateurs has worked to clear German food of its stodgy reputation, trailblazing the way to an inventive, seasonally driven culinary style that has been dubbed "New German".

Try it at **Volt**, a chic restaurant by the canal in Kreuzberg, where the forward-thinking fare is matched by edgy décor. Housed in a refurbished electricity transformer station, the venue features soaring ceilings, exposed brick and rows of gleaming copper lamps to accompany the contemporary offerings. The chef updates classic eats with clever twists and daring combinations, such as confit of black feathered chicken with peppers, mozzarella and lovage, and one of the five-course menus always caters to vegetarians.

Also taking advantage of a post-industrial location is **Eins44**. Ensconced in a Neukölln courtyard, the eatery has transformed a tiled hall once used as a distillery into a trendy spot for upscale German food with dashes of French influence. The fare here changes frequently to take advantage of whatever's fresh at the markets – look out for delish offerings like duck, cod and ox.

The celebrated chef at **Martha's** in Schöneberg gets even more innovative, incorporating all sorts of far-flung ingredients like kelp, miso and amaranth. The "Martha's Special" section of the menu features a schmorgericht (roasted or braised pork, beef or veal) grounded in local comfort food, though even there you'll find dashes of fusion flair. Every meal starts with a warm slab of bread studded with chunks of blood sausage, a carnivorous specialty that has won me over.

A more down-to-earth take on German food is the focus at **Föllerei**, a snug, welcoming locale decorated simply with portraits of hunters. I used to live down the street, and when I moved, leaving Föllerei was one of my biggest regrets. The spread changes daily, playing around with seasonal ingredients without straying far from homey tradition, and every dish just tastes like it was prepared with love.

Herz & Niere is another place rooted in Germany's rustic roots. The name, which means "Heart and Kidney," should give a hint as to what's in store; the chefs take the nose-to-tail approach of using every part of the animal, from pig to cow to fowl. Never fear – there are also prix fixe menus for vegetarians and the offal-shy. This is a daring and delicious approach to making something new by reviving cooking traditions long forgotten.

friedrichshain

No other part of the capital is as full of contrasts as Friedrichshain. While it keeps one foot firmly planted in its punk, alternative past, it also buzzes with new development and a thriving nightlife scene. The squat houses have mostly been edged out by spiffy condominium developments, but street art and subculture are still here in spades. There are a few ways to get to this eastern district, but I'd recommend crossing the Spree River via the red-bricked Oberbaum Bridge, which lands you right on raucous Warschauer Strasse. Straight ahead and to the right will be the two liveliest parts of the neighborhood. There's the sprawling, graffiti-covered brick warehouses of the RAW complex on Revaler Strasse, a former train yard that's now home to cafés, clubs, flea markets, a swimming pool and even a skate park and climbing wall. A bit farther ahead, the bars and restaurants around Simon-Dach-Strasse and Boxhagener Platz come alive every night of the week.

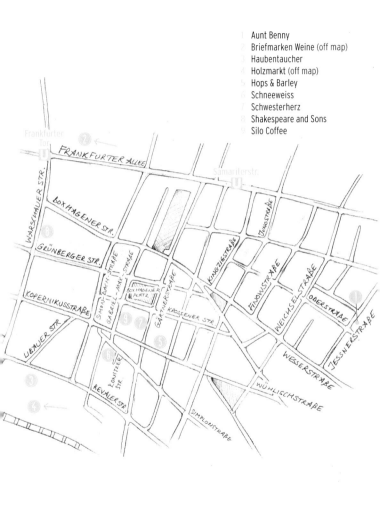

AUNT BENNY

Cake, quiche and coffee – Canadian style

Oderstrasse 7 (at Jessnerstrasse) / **+49 30 6640 5300**
auntbenny.com / **Closed Monday**

This is exactly the kind of café I love, with delectable food both sweet and savory and a fetching yet chilled-out space. The only thing I can fault it for is being so far from where I live. Specials are scrawled on a big, wall-sized chalkboard and large windows create a bright and welcoming mood. With its Canadian owners, Aunt Benny's menu is more international than your average local outfit, with a variety of lip-smacking sandwiches and quiches. The real imperative, however, is getting yourself a piece of the incredible carrot cake before it sells out.

BRIEFMARKEN WEINE

Retro Italian wine bar

Karl-Marx-Allee 99 (near Strasse der Pariser Kommune)
+49 30 4202 5293   briefmarkenweine.de   Closed Sunday

A former stamp collector's shop has been transformed into an inviting neighborhood drinking nook that positively glows with historic charm and warmth. Knowing that they had stumbled upon a special space, the two Italian owners preserved the lustrous wooden cabinets, scrolled wallpaper and old-school neon sign out front that still spells out "briefmarken" (stamps). The location adds to the special ambiance too, set on a monumental East Berlin boulevard lined with Stalinist architecture. Choose from a broad spectrum of beguiling drops, paired with an inviting antipasti platter with prosciutto, fresh mozzarella and marinated artichokes, or the daily pasta special, made with whatever was freshest at the market.

HAUBENTAUCHER

Pool lounge in an unexpected venue

Revaler Strasse 99 (near Libauer Strasse) / +49 30 297 766 770
haubentaucher.berlin / Open daily late April to September

On hot summer days, when most folks are looking for a lake to take a dip, the hip crowd is heading to Haubentaucher. With its expansive pool, beach bar, chill-out lounge areas and occasional DJ appearances, there's a bit of an LA pool party vibe going on, though the post-industrial setting in a former railway yard adds that special Berlin touch. There are yoga classes offered on the poolside deck on some mornings, though the hedonists arrive later in the day for a swim and a sunset cocktail. The pool is open from late April to September, but throughout the year, the venue hosts parties, concerts, festivals and markets.

HOLZMARKT

Food and fun down by the river

Holzmarktstrasse 19-30 (near Krautstrasse)
+49 30 4736 1686 / holzmarkt.com / Closed Monday

Holzmarkt comes from a pretty legendary pedigree. This cool, ramshackle village on the banks of the Spree is from the same crew that used to run Bar25 down the road, one of the most notorious homegrown clubs of the 2000s. Today's Holzmarkt is a complex of buildings and spaces that carries on the free-spirited legacy of its predecessor. On the premises are the Fame Restaurant, which serves Swiss fondue and stays cozy through winter with a wooden hut, plus the Kater Blau club, which throws parties every weekend and hosts events like flea markets, concerts, theater performances and film screenings. In the summer, watching the sunset from the Pampa beach bar is a must.

HOPS & BARLEY

Booze up

Wühlischstrasse 22-23 (near Gärtnerstrasse) / +49 30 2936 7534
hopsandbarley.eu / Open daily

Take note, beer lovers. The owner of this microbrewery-cum-bar is a real-deal, certified master brewer, and unlike many of his German brewer brethren, he likes to get experimental, playing around with different varieties of hops and malt to create limited-edition beverages. Always on tap are the house pilsner, a malty-sweet dark beer (the Friedrichshain Dark, which includes four types of Bavarian malt) and a light and fruity wheat beer, plus two rotating special brews, all of which are served unfiltered for the proper full-bodied microbrew taste experience. There's even a crisp small-batch apple cider. Old-fashioned tiles still adorn the walls, remnants of the space's former life as a family-run butcher shop.

SCHNEEWEISS

Austrian cuisine with a touch of elegance

Simplonstrasse 16 (at Konitzer Strasse)   +49 30 2904 9704
schneeweiss-berlin.de / Open daily

With its top-to-bottom all-white décor, the look at Schneeweiss is
reminiscent of snow-capped Alpine peaks. The cuisine is of that region
too, with Austrian standards like beef goulash with dumplings and
apple strudel in addition to more contemporary fusion dishes that center
around the season's finest ingredients. I recommend sticking with the
traditional side of the menu: thin, tender and perfectly golden-crisp,
the schnitzel is a masterpiece. Afterward, get comfy in the lounge at the
back, which features a fireplace and a chic après-ski vibe, to sip a glass of
Austria's post-dinner digestif, apricot brandy.

SCHWESTERHERZ

Gorgeous pleasures

Gärtnerstrasse 28 (near Wühlischstrasse) / **+49 30 7790 1183**
schwesterherz-berlin.de / **Closed Sunday**

With all sorts of attractive paper goods and lovable home accessories, Schwesterherz makes for joyful, endless browsing. There are so many things to discover: reams of gift wrap with eye-catching prints, hand-stitched notebooks with colorfully printed covers, vintage-style posters, wooden toys, letterpress cards and home décor items like marble candleholders and copper storage jars. It's the kind of place that reminds you to include touches of beauty in everyday life. For even more design inspiration, the sister shop right next door, Küchenliebe, is dedicated to things for the home cook, with pretty glassware, crockery, old-fashioned utensils and cookbooks to pore over.

SHAKESPEARE AND SONS

One-stop shop for books, bagels and coffee

Warschauerstrasse 74 (near Grünberger Strasse)
+49 30 4000 3685 / shakesbooks.de / Open daily

Books and bagels: a dream combo if there ever was one. Czech-born Roman looks after the literary side of things, and named the bookstore after the legendary Shakespeare and Company shop in Paris, where he once worked. His American wife, Laurel, is the force behind the authentic New York-style bagels served in the shop's café, which are boiled before baking to make 'em nice and chewy in accordance with her Jewish grandmother's recipe. Sink your teeth into a poppy seed bagel smeared thickly with cream cheese and topped with lox before browsing the great curation of English books, including titles by expat writers living here.

SILO COFFEE

From Melbourne, with love

Gabriel-Max-Strasse 4 (near Krossener Strasse) / +49 30 7407 8746
silo-coffee.com / Open daily

The two Aussie cousins behind Silo were some of the very first to introduce Berliners to the trendy cafés of their homeland. With wooden tables, lots of exposed brick and coffee cups in an eye-catching lipstick red, the aesthetics of the place are flawless. As is the really good coffee, from that Down Under essential, the flat white, to bottles of smooth yet potent cold brew. But what really catapults Silo into the superstar stratosphere is their brunch menu that features delectable treats like oven-baked pancakes served in mini cast-iron skillets, or poached eggs on sourdough with avocado and bacon.

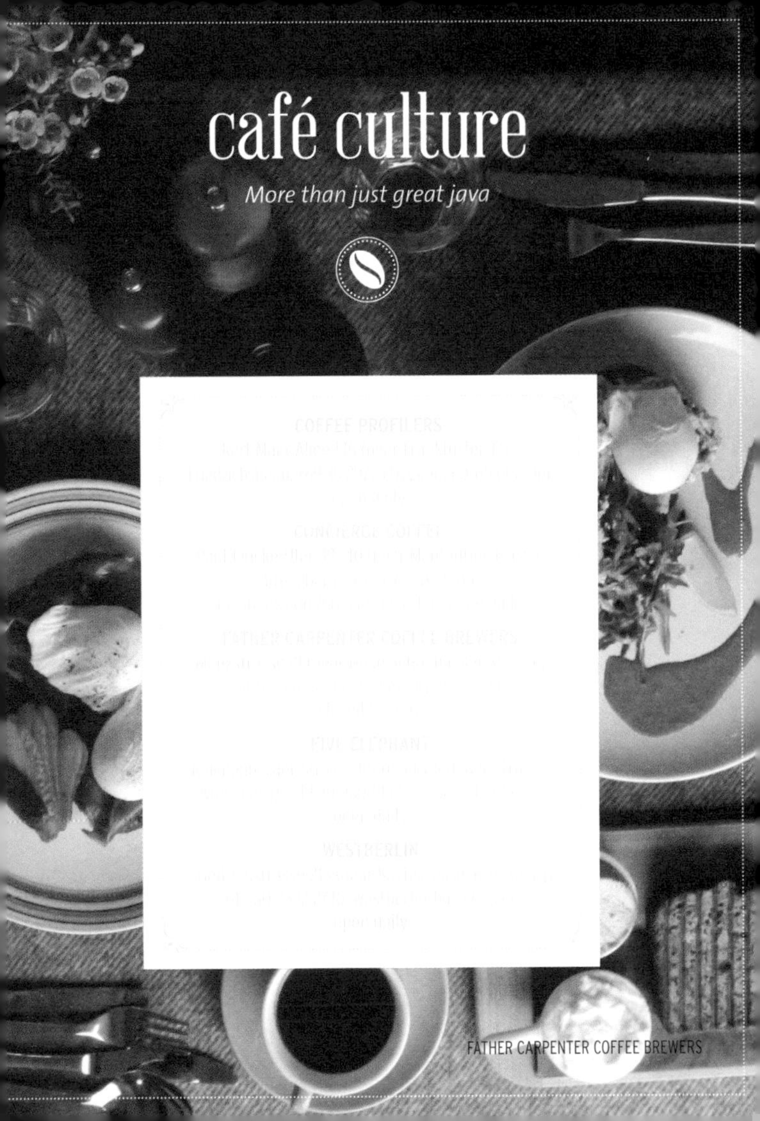

café culture

More than just great java

COFFEE PROFILERS

CUMULUS COFFEE

FATHER CARPENTER COFFEE BREWERS

FINK ELEPHANT

WESTERLIND

In recent years, Berlin has seriously upped its coffee game. Once a rarity here, an exceptional cup has become the new standard, and stylish, quality-focused cafés have popped up all over town.

A long-time personal favorite is **Five Elephant**, a compact and perpetually busy hangout near the bottom of Kreuzberg's Görlitzer Park. Beans are sourced from small-scale farmers in Ethiopia and South America and roasted on-site before being brewed up by expert baristas. The essential accompaniment to every drink is a wedge of Five Elephant's famous (and addictive) Philly-style cheesecake, made according to a top-secret recipe from the owner's grandma.

Ensconced in a stunning brick courtyard, just a few steps from Mitte's trendiest shopping neighborhood, **Father Carpenter Coffee Brewers** seamlessly combines good looks with fine brews, not to mention fresh juices, brioche sandwiches and a brunch menu served until late afternoon. The subdued, utilitarian-chic décor inside is admittedly lovely, but when the weather's nice, the really coveted seats are the ones out in the peaceful courtyard.

Also oozing with charm is Kreuzberg's **Concierge Coffee**, wedged into a tight passageway room that was originally designed for the building's porter. Place your order right at the cute green window and get it to go, then enjoy your cappuccino or flat white next to the canal that ambles by on the other side of the street.

Coffee Profilers is another café that takes advantage of a unique location, with enormous glass windows looking out onto Friedrichshain's Karl-Marx-Allee. From a seat out on the wide sidewalk, you're well positioned to take in the striking Stalinist architecture of this East German boulevard. All the beans are sourced from an exacting Greek roaster and brewed according to equally rigorous standards. The pour-overs on offer are especially impressive.

Westberlin is more than just a coffee shop – it's also a magazine shop stocking a mix of niche and picturesque periodicals. With the owner being an architect, the space has a stylish, minimalist layout with a thoughtful mix of contemporary furniture. In addition to the great coffee, a delectable array of sandwiches, quiches and cakes, along with plenty of seating make this a memorable pit stop just a stone's throw from hectic, touristy Checkpoint Charlie.

WESTBERLIN

prenzlauer berg

Tranquil and somewhat yuppie, Prenzlauer Berg is a family-friendly area with parks, playgrounds and cafés galore. Berliners joke that this is the neighborhood of expensive strollers and, well, it's pretty much true. In the '80s and '90s, it was the epicenter of East Berlin's rebellious art and music scenes. Today, the only remaining signs that this was part of the East are that trams still run here (West Berlin dismantled its tram network) and pedestrian crossing lights still feature the Ampelmann figure. With lots of leafy streets, Art Nouveau buildings and upscale eateries, Prenzlauer Berg is incredibly pleasant and a good destination for dining but less so for nightlife. A stroll up Kastanienallee will yield shopping options aplenty, while the streets around Kollwitzplatz and Helmholtzplatz are appealing spots to soak up the local life.

1 Bryk Bar
2 Chutnify
3 Eispatisserie Hokey Pokey
4 Lichtblick-Kino
5 Meierei
6 Omoni (off map)
7 Rawtastic
8 Scandinavian Objects
9 VEB Orange (off map)
10 Victoria Met Albert

BRYK BAR

Smart cocktail joint

Rykestrasse 18 (near Sredzkistrasse) / +49 30 3810 0165
bryk-bar.com / Closed Sunday

"Black has it all. [Its] beauty is absolute," the legendary Coco Chanel
once said. Bryk has followed her style credo, cladding its bar, walls
and velvet armchairs all in black, and the result is a fittingly striking
backdrop for their manifesto of "avant-garde drinking". A cornerstone
of the incredibly original menu is spin-offs of the gin and tonic using
their own line of limited-edition Bryk Gin, which comes in black bottles,
of course. The Earl of Berlin is my kind of drink: Earl Grey tea-infused
Bryk Gin, topped with bitter lemonade and garnished with a slice
of cucumber.

CHUTNIFY

Bring on the spice

Sredzkistrasse 43 (near Husemannstrasse) / **+49 30 4401 0795**
chutnify.com / **Closed Monday**

Germans are generally pretty spice averse, but Chutnify is out to
challenge those lame taste buds. I've long been an Indian food fan,
so I was definitely happy when this upstart opened in late 2014 to shake
up the city's dull South Asian offerings. The house specialty is dosas:
thin and crispy rice-lentil crêpes filled with saucy vegetarian or meat
curries. I can vouch for both the masala potato and Goan pork as being
pretty damn tasty, especially when topped up with as much spicy
chutney as you can handle.

EISPATISSERIE HOKEY POKEY

We all scream for ice cream

Stargarder Strasse 73 (near Pappelallee) / **+49 176 8010 3080**
hokey-pokey.de / **Open daily**

There is often a line snaking tens of meters down the sidewalk, but that
doesn't deter anyone. It certainly has never deterred me. The unbelievably
mouth-watering homemade treat served here is well worth any wait.
The array of extravagant and oftentimes creative flavors is updated
regularly, though the namesake Hokey Pokey is always on hand: rich vanilla
studded with golden honeycomb toffee bits. I could never pick just one,
though the banana-chocolate-peanut butter and luscious Sicilian pistachio
are both up there as frontrunners. Three words: To. Die. For.

LICHTBLICK-KINO

Tiny indie cinema

Kastanienallee 77 (near Schwedter Strasse) / **+49 30 4405 8179**
lichtblick-kino.org / **Open daily**

I love going out to see movies, but I can't stand multiplex movie theaters. Being packed into rows of seats by the hundreds makes me feel like I'm on an airplane. With only 32 seats and a program that steers firmly away from anything too Hollywood or blockbuster, Lichtblick-Kino is the very antithesis of those giant, soulless venues. They play a mix of documentaries, local indies, small festival darlings, foreign films and classics. In a longstanding tradition that I find incredibly romantic, every Saturday at midnight the theater screens *Casablanca*, the 1942 love story of an irascible Humphrey Bogart and a radiant Ingrid Bergman torn apart by war. "Here's looking at you, kid..."

MEIEREI

Alpine eats

**Kollwitzstrasse 42 (near Belforter Strasse) / +49 30 9212 9573
meierei.net / Open daily**

There's just something so irresistibly wholesome about the Alps,
isn't there? Fresh air, green meadows, tinkling cowbells and cheese,
delicious cheese... Meierei is all about rib-sticking comfort food for urban
mountaineers, served from the early breakfast hours until late lunch.
The essential mountain breakfast looks something like Bircher müsli or
Weisswurst, wobbly white veal sausages that are especially relished in
Bavaria. Later in the day, you could use some rich ox goulash, Spätzle
noodles with melted cheese and apple strudel for dessert. After all, it's
been a long, hard day tending to your cowherd up on the mountainside.

omoni

Calling all sushi lovers

Kopenhagener Strasse 14 (near Sonnenburger Strasse)
+49 30 2361 9244 / No website / Closed Monday

It isn't exactly easy to find Omoni, which is hidden down a quiet residential street and doesn't have a sign out front. Then again, it isn't exactly easy to get great sushi in this city, and I'm of the opinion that Omoni is unrivaled, so it's definitely worth the trek — I regularly travel all the way across town to get my fix. There are some Korean rice dishes on the menu, but skip those and go for any of the mixed sushi and sashimi sets. It's clear just how incredibly fresh the fish is upon first bite.

RAWTASTIC

Meat-free, heat-free cooking

Danziger Strasse 16 (near Hagenauer Strasse) / +49 172 439 1287
rawtastic.de / Open daily

Life is all about balance, right? Some days, it's a juicy, charbroiled burger I crave, and on others, healthy veggie stuff. Rawtastic, the first all-raw, all-vegan restaurant here, is out to convince Berliners that you don't need heat, meat or dairy to eat well. I must confess I was a bit skeptical the first time I tried raw cuisine, but actually found it tasty, filling, and of course, super fresh. Because everything is prepared and served cold or room temperature, the chefs had to get truly inventive, dreaming up plates like tacos filled with spicy walnut "meat" and lasagna with layers of marinated zucchini and nut "cheese".

SCANDINAVIAN OBJECTS

Impeccable home goods from up north

Rykestrasse 31 (near Danziger Strasse) / +49 30 4849 5626
scandinavianobjects.com / Closed Sunday and Monday

What is it about the Scandinavians? It seems like they have the golden touch when it comes to design. From furniture to toys to a plethora of useful things around the home, everything they make up there seems to call my name. For that reason, an excursion to the Scandinavian Objects store is a bit dangerous — for my bank balance at least. It's hard to resist the pretty teacup sets, vases and candleholders, not to mention the iconic String shelves in a rainbow of colors and hanging lamps by legendary Finnish designer Alvar Aalto, plated in gleaming chrome or brass.

VEB ORANGE

Colorful kitsch

Oderberger Strasse 29 (near Schwedter Strasse)
+49 30 9788 6886 / veborange.de / Closed Sunday

It's the rule of thumb in trends: wait long enough and eventually any
given thing will end up in style again. It's taken a few decades, but the
stuff at VEB Orange, in all its bright plastic glory, is now the epitome
of retro cool. From polyester outfits to pleather armchairs, crockery,
collectibles, alarm clocks and fabulous light fixtures, the shop is so
crammed with everyday objects from East German life, it feels like
a time capsule of an era and country from the not-so-distant past.

VICTORIA MET ALBERT

The shop with something for everyone

Dunckerstrasse 81 (at Lettestrasse) / **+49 30 4467 4772**
victoriametalbert.com / **Closed Sunday**

The pair behind this corner shop – he a Londoner, she a Berliner – took the unlikely love story of British Queen Victoria and German Prince Albert as their inspiration. Combining their differing backgrounds and aesthetic influences, they've assembled an irresistible hodgepodge of fashion, accessories and housewares that blends cool elegance with shabby chic. From the fun little toys to Scrabble tile mugs, English wool sweaters to embroidered throw pillows, this is the kind of retail heaven where I find so many things I love, I start racking my brain for people I know with birthdays coming up. One for them, one for me: just my kind of gift shopping.

cheers to beer

Where to imbibe

BERGSCHLOSS
Kopfstrasse 59 (near Morusstrasse; Neukölln)
+49 30 6443 5906, berlinerberg.com
open Thursday through Saturday

HOPFENREICH
Sorauer Strasse 31 (at Wrangelstrasse; Kreuzberg)
+49 30 8806 1080, hopfenreich.de, open daily

KURHAUS PONTE ROSA
Kreuzbergstrasse 42B (at Monumentenstrasse;
Kreuzberg), +49 30 7871 2244, kurhaus-ponte-rosa.de
open daily April through September

LAGER LAGER
Pflügerstrasse 68 (near Liberdastrasse; Neukölln)
+49 30 2390 3919, lagerlagerberlin.de
closed Sunday

PFEFFERBRÄU
Schönhauser Allee 176 (near Fehrbelliner Strasse;
Prenzlauer Berg), +49 30 473 773 6240
pfefferbraeu.de, closed Monday

Berliners have been brewing and quaffing for centuries, and with beer being as deeply woven as it is in the culture, there is no shortage of places to drink up throughout the city.

One of my preferred beer gardens is more off the beaten track, though: tucked away next to a stretch of disused railroad on the western edge of Kreuzberg and ringed by trees, **Kurhaus Ponte Rosa** is a small, friendly outfit that feels like a secret neighborhood locale. Besides the all-important brews, the house specialty is thin-crust pizza from a wood-fired oven.

Though you usually find a selection of commercial brands on tap here, there are also numerous microbreweries making their own inventive drinks. One of them is Neukölln's Berliner Berg, which has its own **Bergschloss** taproom, a comfortable spot with antique wooden floors and antiquated furniture. There are always several Berliner Berg boozes on tap, like a fruity pale ale and a potent imperial stout, as well as kegs from other local craft brewers.

Another microbrewery is **Pfefferbräu**, which occupies a hilltop location in Prenzlauer Berg, and was established in 1893. The enormous copper kettles pump out a light pilsner, a dunkel (malty dark brew) and an unfiltered wheat with whiffs of passion fruit, all of which can be enjoyed inside or out on the terrace along with a broad menu of snacks and meals.

Hopfenreich doesn't make its own beer, but what it offers instead is an unbelievable variety. With 15 or more kegs on tap at any given time and a bevy of bottles from around the globe, the Kreuzberg watering hole boasts what is quite likely the largest craft beer selection in town. Even the most dedicated connoisseurs are sure to discover something new and surprising.

Lager Lager is part bar, part shop. Bottles and drafts can be sampled on site or packed up for home, and this is the only place here that sells craft beer to go in growlers.

wedding

Slightly scruffy and still up-and-coming, Wedding today is what Kreuzberg was in the early 2000s. It's been predicted to become Berlin's next big thing for some years already, and though that's yet to totally take off, the affordability and availability of real estate here keeps attracting lots of students and artists. There's still plenty of space for people to let their creative ideas unfold, which means it will be full of surprises for some time to come. There isn't much in terms of interesting shopping, but more and more drinking establishments, restaurants and cafés are opening all the time. There are things to see and do around Gesundbrunnen on the U8 U-Bahn line, but most of the action is clustered along the U6 line, in the side streets on either side off busy Müllerstrasse. Climb to the top of Humboldthain Park for some amazing cityscape views.

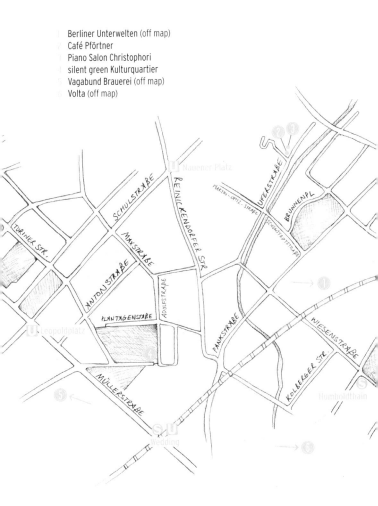

BERLINER UNTERWELTEN

Underground adventures

Brunnenstrasse 105 (near Ramlerstrasse) / +49 30 4991 0517
berliner-unterwelten.de / Tour times vary

This city has many layers of history to experience, and Berliner Unterwelten offers a perspective like none other. A non-profit association, they are dedicated to preserving subterranean spaces to ensure these hidden, neglected stories from the city's past will still be around for future generations. The two main tours they offer (and the central ticket office) are here in Wedding, including a thrilling exploration of a labyrinthine WWII air raid shelter below Gesundbrunnen station, where civilians hid from Allied bombs. Or, descend into a massive Nazi anti-aircraft gun tower that was so indestructible, it was simply buried after the war.

CAFÉ PFÖRTNER

Delish meals on (bus) wheels

Uferstrasse 8-11 (near Martin-Opitz-Strasse) / **+49 30 5036 9854**
pfoertner.co / Closed Sunday

The best food in Wedding is served at Pförtner. You've got a choice of
seating: inside, where the porter had his office back when this space was
a train workshop, or outside in the school bus, where table setups have
replaced the bus seats. Both the lunch and dinner menus are refreshed
daily, grounded in Italian cooking but with liberal touches from German
and international cuisines. Count on rustic dishes that are elevated to
another level by fresh ingredients and careful attention to detail. If there's
seafood pasta on the menu, you've hit the jackpot. After dinner, head next
door for a concert at Piano Salon Christophori (pg 92), and you'll have the
perfect date night.

PIANO SALON CHRISTOPHORI

Magical concerts in an unlikely setting

Uferstrasse 8 (near Martin-Opitz-Strasse) / **No phone**
konzertfluegel.com / **Check website for schedules**

I'm ashamed to admit it, but the younger me occasionally fell asleep at classical music performances. That all changed, however, when I discovered the gem that is Piano Salon Christophori. In a brick warehouse where subway cars were once repaired, professional pianists play informal, intimate shows to an audience perched on mismatched couches and chairs. By day, the space is a workshop for restoring rare pianos, but by night, under the glow of vintage chandeliers, it comes alive with music and romance. That special Berlin touch: tickets are donation based, as is the self-serve wine bar.

SILENT GREEN KULTURQUARTIER

From crematorium to cultural center

**Gerichtstrasse 35 (at Adolfstrasse) / +49 30 4606 7324
silent-green.net / Savvy Contemporary art gallery closed Monday
and Tuesday, Moos Restaurant open daily**

It might seem a bit morbid to hang out at a former crematorium, but the
past life of this place only lends to its special ambiance. Walking up the
long lawn toward the cluster of pointed stone buildings feels like a scene
out of a Gothic horror story, and the looming smokestack only adds to the
eerie feel. Since 2013, the long-since-disused site has been a mixed-use
creative quarter hosting regular concerts, exhibitions, performances and
other cultural events. Permanent residents include the Moos Restaurant,
a gorgeous, light-filled venue serving contemporary European cuisine and
drinks every day, and the Savvy Contemporary, an art gallery with a variety
of multidisciplinary projects.

VAGABUND BRAUEREI

American beer pioneers

Antwerpener Strasse 3 (near Seestrasse) / +49 30 5266 7668
vagabundbrauerei.com / Open daily

Back in 2011, unusual, international craft brews were a rarity in this city. Fed up with the limited options, a trio of American friends decided to start brewing their own – making it on such a small scale that they designated themselves not a microbrewery, but a nanobrewery. The taproom they opened in 2013 quickly established itself as one of Wedding's most-loved drinking establishments, where fans can imbibe Vagabund's own brews – ranging from robust porters and smoked ales to the award-winning Szechuan Saison, pepped up with coriander seeds and peppercorns – as well as an array of special bottles sourced from around the globe.

VOLTA

Fun, contemporary dining

Brunnenstrasse 73 (near Demminer Strasse) | **+49 176 7755 6422**
dasvolta.com | Closed Sunday

On a somewhat desolate block in a rather unsightly 1970s building,
Volta has managed to carve out an edgy restaurant and establish itself as
one of the leading eateries around. With raw concrete walls, exposed piping
overhead and a low-lit interior pierced by some dangling purple lights,
Volta feels almost more like an underground club than an eatery   until the
food arrives. That will be inventive, playful international cuisine with lots of
fusion-y Asian touches, like pork belly blinis, Korean chicken wings and the
famous Volta burger, which comes on a poppyseed bun and is with made
with Black Angus beef and topped with cheddar, barbecue sauce, sauerkraut,
Spreewald pickles, rucola, tomato and bacon. Make sure to save room for an
enormous ice cream sandwich for dessert.

BERLIN AFTER DARK:
stand-out cocktail bars

The city's finest tipples

BUCK AND BRECK
Brunnenstrasse 177 (near Invalidenstrasse; Mitte)
+49 176 3231 5507, buckandbreck.com, open daily

GREEN DOOR
Winterfeldtstrasse 50 (near Goltzstrasse;
Schöneberg), +49 30 215 2515, greendoor.de
open daily

THE BAR MARQUÉS
Graefestrasse 92 (near Planufer; Kreuzberg)
+49 30 6162 5906, facebook.com/The-Bar-Marqués
open daily

TIER
Weserstrasse 42 (at Fuldastrasse; Neukölln)
no phone, facebook.com/TierBar, open daily

WÜRGEENGEL
Dresdener Strasse 122 (near Oranienplatz;
Kreuzberg), +49 30 615 5560, wuergeengel.de
open daily

There's certainly no shortage of watering holes in Berlin but for a truly exceptional cocktail, it's worth making the effort to explore someplace special. One of my all-time picks is **Würgeengel**, a Kreuzberg old-timer that well predates the current artisanal mixed drink trend. With burgundy walls, velvet banquettes and dim chandeliers, the look is dark and sultry, and the bartenders are real pros. There's just something about the vibe here that makes me want whiskey (not to mention a cigarette, though I quit years ago) so my standard order is an Old Fashioned.

A short stroll away is **The Bar Marqués**, a rather hidden speakeasy in the basement of a tapas restaurant. Go for the tip-top drinks and ambiance. The intimate venue is styled like a Colonial Era gentlemen's club, with leather stools and plush armchairs you can pull up to the fireplace. The specialty is creative mixology, but I recommend taking inspiration from the colonial theme and going for a G&T with a unique house twist.

Trendy Neukölln is well known for its abundance of bars, but **Tier** stands out from the pack. In fact, I wager they make the top drinks in the neighborhood. That also makes them regularly packed, but it's worth squeezing in to try a libation (or three) and to mingle with the hipster crowd, rosemary gimlet in hand.

For a taste of the cocktail scene in a more grown-up part of town, Schöneberg's **Green Door** is it. After ringing the bell and gaining entry, you'll find yourself in a slick, retro-styled bar with a touch of 1970s kitsch. Green Door commands a certain respect: at more than two decades old, it's one of the elders in the bar scene. Your order (go for the Old Cuban, made with gold rum, Angostura bitters, lime juice, simple syrup, mint and sparkling wine) may take some time to arrive, but your patience will be handsomely rewarded.

Easily the most niche boozing spot in the city is Mitte's **Buck and Breck**, a teeny place tucked behind an anonymous storefront with only 14 seats. Once they're taken, all the unlucky souls who ring the doorbell (simply marked "Bar") get turned away. Inside, the seats are ringed around the all-black bar where the bartender works his magic, mixing up each drink (bespoke, if you so desire) with the passion and precision of a true mixology master.

THE BAR MARQUÉS

BERLIN AFTER DARK:
sounds of the city

Get your groove on

MADAME CLAUDE
Lübbener Strasse 19 (near Wrangelstrasse),
Kreuzberg; +49 30 840 0859, madameclaude.de
open daily

PRIVATCLUB
Skalitzer Strasse 85-86 (near Zeughofstrasse),
Kreuzberg; +49 30 6117 9362, privatclub-berlin.de
open daily

S036
Oranienstrasse 190 (near Manteuffelstrasse),
Kreuzberg; +49 30 6140 1306, so36.de
several concerts per week

WHITE TRASH FAST FOOD
Am Flutgraben 2 (at Puschkinallee), Kreuzberg;
+49 30 351 500 587, whitetrashfastfood.com
open daily

YORCKSCHLÖSSCHEN
Yorckstrasse 15 (near Grossbeerenstrasse),
Kreuzberg; +49 30 215 8070, yorckschloesschen.de
open daily

PRIVATCLUB

When people ask why I love living in Berlin, my first reason is that there's so much going on here: you could truly go out any and every night of the week and always have a fantastic time. Music is a prominent dish in the local cultural smorgasbord, and venues abound with concerts of all styles and genres. **SO36** counts as one of the legends. In the '70s and '80s, it was the core of Kreuzberg's wild punk and new wave scene, hosting legends such as Dead Kennedys, Suicide and Einstürzende Neubauten. These days, SO36 has expanded its repertoire to such genres as rock and Balkan beats, and even holds roller disco parties.

Smaller but definitely worth a visit is **Madame Claude**, also in Kreuzberg. Descending the stairs into the basement performance space, things start feeling a bit topsy-turvy – that's because an entire living room's worth of furniture has been attached upside down to the ceiling, and you might have to remind yourself which way is up as the evening goes on. The nightly performances feature many homegrown unknowns, and the weekly Experimontag and Freaky Friday nights are a treasure trove of weird, genre-defying stuff.

White Trash Fast Food is another venue with an irreverent edge. Combining restaurant, beer garden and tattoo studio with a concert stage,

White Trash hosts nightly shows where you can chow down on a fat burger while being serenaded with something loud and live. In keeping with the place's rowdy, rockabilly theme, the shows have a solid rock and punk bent.

With Berlin being the techno haven that it is, I've often had friends ask where they can go out dancing to music that isn't electronic. My response is always **Privatclub**. There are concerts nearly every night of the week featuring mellow singer-songwriter stuff to indie bands with a lively pop beat, and on the weekends, the floor fills up with partygoers dancing to boogie, soul and hip-hop sounds.

There are jazz clubs dotting the city, but **Yorckschlösschen** is something remarkable. An easygoing corner pub in western Kreuzberg, it dates back more than 100 years, making it one of the oldest pubs in the city. For the past 40 or so years, owner Olaf has been inviting jazz, blues and swing acts to play three to five nights a week. It's an utterly unpretentious place to have a bite, a drink and catch some grooves, an atmosphere borrowed from the jazz joints of New Orleans's French Quarter.

schöneberg and tiergarten

Schöneberg was the epicenter of Berlin's famously wild bar and cabaret scenes in the 1920s, with Nollendorfplatz in particular becoming the hub of gay and lesbian nightlife in the German capital, if not the world. Things aren't quite as rowdy as they were in those heady days, although some great cocktail joints, as well as a thriving gay scene, still call the area home. Over the years, Schöneberg has grown into a charming residential neighborhood. The cluster of streets between Nollendorfplatz and Eisenacher Strasse is one of my preferred places for a weekend stroll, and there's lots to discover on Goltzstrasse. Just a stone's throw away in the neighboring Tiergarten area, a compact art district has popped up on Potsdamer Strasse with renowned galleries and experience-focused retail stores. The sprawling Tiergarten Park extends over this entire section of the city, offering tranquil walks and shaded beer gardens.

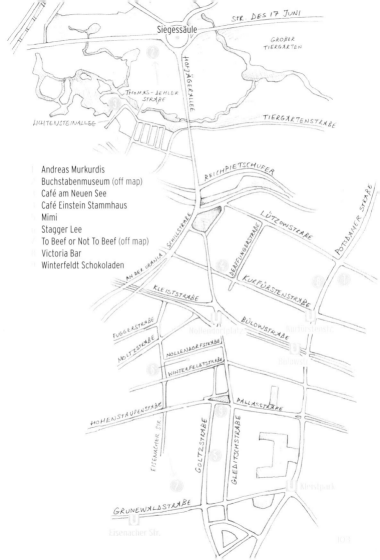

Siegessäule

STR. DES 17 JUNI

GROßER TIERGARTEN

HOFJÄGERALLEE

THOMAS-DEHLER STRAßE

LICHTENSTEINALLEE

TIERGARTENSTRAßE

REICHPIETSCHUFER

LÜTZOWSTRAßE

POTSDAMER STRAßE

SCHILLSTRAßE

DERFFLINGERSTRAßE

KURFÜRSTENSTRAßE

AN DER URANIA

KLEISTSTRAßE

BÜLOWSTRAßE

Nollendorfplatz · Nollendorfstr.

Kurfürstenstr.

Bülowstr.

FUGGERSTRAßE

MOLTZSTRAßE

NOLLENDORFSTRAßE

WINTERFELDTSTRAßE

DALLASSTRAßE

HOHENSTAUFENSTRAßE

EISENACHER STR.

GOLTZSTRAßE

GLEDITSCHSTRAßE

Kleistpark

GRUNEWALDSTRAßE

Eisenacher Str.

Andreas Murkurdis
Buchstabenmuseum (off map)
Café am Neuen See
Café Einstein Stammhaus
Mimi
Stagger Lee
To Beef or Not To Beef (off map)
Victoria Bar
Winterfeldt Schokoladen

ANDREAS MURKURDIS

Tightly curated fashion and lifestyle finds

Potsdamer Strasse 81E (near Lützowstrasse) / **+49 30 680 798 306**
andreasmurkudis.com / Closed Sunday

Concept shops are a well-worn retail model these days, but Andreas Murkudis was a local forerunner. Since as early as 2003, this has been a go-to shopping destination for Berliners with exquisite taste. Formerly in Mitte, the store moved to its current location in 2011, a huge, airy space (previously a printing press for the *Tagesspiegel* newspaper) that provides a starkly white, gallery-like backdrop for the carefully sourced wares. Besides sleek fashion for men, women and even children, the collection includes perfumes, jewelry, eyewear, aesthetic objects for the home and a full range of Australia's coveted skincare brand, Aesop.

BUCHSTABENMUSEUM

From A to Z

Stadtbahnbogen 424 (at Claudiusstrasse) / +49 177 420 1587
buchstabenmuseum.de / Open Friday and Saturday

Let's hear it for all the letters of the alphabet – they're the building blocks
that make so much of our communication possible. Buchstabenmuseum is
a quirky, non-profit institution passionately devoted to saving Berlin's most
prominent signs – that is, those that have marked the city's shops and public
spaces for generations. Rescuing many of these dismantled fonts just before
they're sent to the junkyard, the museum has amassed a collection of more
than 1,000 characters and words, from flamboyant cursive to no-nonsense
Helvetica. Paying a visit offers not only an overview of typography throughout
the years, but also a taste of Berlin's urban history.

CAFÉ AM NEUEN SEE

Bucolic waterside biergarten

Lichtensteinallee 2 (at Thomas-Dehler-Strasse) / **+49 30 254 4930**
cafeamneuensee.de / **Open daily**

This is such a pastoral location, it's hard to believe it's right in the center of the city. Next to a small lake on the southwest edge of Tiergarten Park, Café am Neuen See is a restaurant, beer garden and waterside hangout in one, a place to escape the urban area without actually having to leave it. Should the weather outside be uninviting, the indoor spots have a cozy ski lodge feel, with antler décor and logs crackling in the fireplace. However, the most pleasant time to come is on a warm, summery day, when the sprawling place is dynamic and bustling, and revelers bob on the sun-dappled lake in rented rowboats.

CAFÉ EINSTEIN STAMMHAUS

Enchanting coffeehouse

Kurfürstenstrasse 58 (near Derfflingerstrasse) / **+49 30 2639 1918**
cafeeinstein.com / **Open daily**

If walls could talk, the ones in Café Einstein would have many stories to tell. This Neo-Renaissance villa was first the home of a wealthy Jewish banker named Georg Blumenfeld, who threw glamorous parties in the 1920s with the socialites and silent film stars of the age. In 1933, the Nazis seized the property to use as an SS outpost. Today, it has been transformed into a dining institution that wouldn't have been out of place in turn-of-the-century Vienna, with gilded walls, marble tabletops and stunning herringbone parquet flooring. It's an exquisite, atmospheric spot for a German-Austrian meal or just some *kaffee* (coffee) and *apfelstrudel* (apple strudel), and the Lebensstern bar upstairs keeps Georg Blumenfeld's party spirit alive.

mimi

The good ol' days of fashion

Goltzstrasse 5 (near Grunewaldstrasse) / **+49 30 2363 8438**
mimi-berlin.de / Closed Sunday

Entering Mimi is like stepping back in time, to an era long before
mass production created today's culture of cheap, throwaway clothing.
The outfits and accessories here are so wonderfully preserved and the
displays so lovingly arranged that calling this a vintage shop doesn't
do it justice, and, in fact, the sign in the window describes these as
"textile antiques". The focus is on clothing from the 1850s to the 1950s,
though the 1920s and 1930s get the most attention. Add a glamorous
beaded Charleston dress and a cloche hat to your wardrobe and let
out your inner flapper. Should there be a special event looming on
your calendar, much of the inventory can also be rented.

STAGGER LEE

Cool bar with excellent drinks

Nollendorfstrasse 27 (near Eisenacher Strasse) / **+49 30 2903 6158**
staggerlee.de / **Open daily**

The actual saloons of the American frontier were probably pretty rough and sleazy, but Stagger Lee has taken the Wild West idea and classed it right up. With burgundy wallpaper, overstuffed leather couches, lots of dark wood, leather-apron-clad bartenders and an old-timey cash register adorning the counter, Stagger Lee is a slick, fun drinking establishment that stays true to its theme while steering well clear of tackiness territory. Many of the impeccable drinks have an Americana slant, like the Alabama Song (bourbon, maple syrup, apple juice, bitters) or the Robert Mitchum (straight-up tequila served with a Lucky Strike). Make sure to try the house specialty, the mint julep, which is kicked up with cherry liqueur and cherry jam.

TO BEEF OR NOT TO BEEF

Steak is the answer

Akazienstrasse 3 (near Hauptstrasse) / +49 30 5459 9047
tobeefornottobeef.berlin / Open daily

Where to find one of the top steaks in town? That is the question.
To Beef or Not To Beef is definitely up for the title, sourcing the most
prime proteins on its menu from celebrity Tuscan butcher Dario Cecchini,
a passionate advocate for the increasingly neglected art of butchery.
The menu features all sorts of beefy pleasures, from carpaccio to
French-style steak frites to burgers, but the restaurant's pride and joy
is the Bistecca alla Fiorentina. This meltingly tender T-bone, one of the
prized, organic cuts imported directly from Chianti, is fittingly described on
the menu as "one of the greatest possible physical pleasures on this earth".

VICTORIA BAR

Swanky cocktail joint

Potsdamer Strasse 102 (near Pohlstrasse) / +49 30 2575 9977
victoriabar.de / Open daily

There's something about perching on a barstool here and nursing a potent
Negroni that makes me feel like I'm a character in an Edward Hopper
painting. Victoria Bar just has that classic 1930s feel to it. Elegant without
being showy, this is the kind of place that will make you want to sit
up straighter to fit in with the polished, grown-up scene. The drinks
menu is exhaustive, but rest assured that whatever you order, the expert,
dapper bartenders will do you right. I recommend the classics, like the
aforementioned Negroni, or a Manhattan.

Cranberry
100g/5.00€

Heidelbeere
100g/5.00€

WINTERFELDT SCHOKOLADEN

For all the chocoholics

Goltzstrasse 23 (at Pallasstrasse) / +49 30 2362 3256
winterfeldt-schokoladen.de / Open daily

As far as addictions go, chocolate is a pretty benign one. So why bother to resist? Winterfeldt Schokoladen is a petite slice of confectionery heaven, housed in a charming corner space that was a pharmacy in a former life. The original wooden cabinets from 1892 are all still intact and as lovely as ever, now repurposed to display the shop's incredible selection of products from around the globe. I like coming here on Saturdays after stocking up at the farmers market just across the road on Winterfeldtplatz. With any luck, I can snag a seat in the back-room café to sip a creamy hot cocoa.

flea markets

Hunting for antiques, art and retro goods

On Sundays, when all the shops stay closed, Berliners get creative on finding ways to spend the day. Passing a couple hours at a flea market is a beloved tradition, offering not only the opportunity to browse and shop, but eat, catch entertainment and get in some lively people-watching as well. Each has its own personality, and there are plenty of one-of-a-kind gems to be found.

Everyone should experience the **Mauerpark Flea Market** at least once. Besides the sheer breadth of things for sale – ranging from East German collectibles to furniture, artwork and clothing made by homegrown designers – its other claim to fame is the enormous outdoor karaoke sessions held in the park amphitheater. Anyone can join the fun for free, so pick a tune and break a leg.

A few blocks away, the **Arkonaplatz Flea Market** is Mauerpark's slightly more sophisticated younger sibling. Though it's smaller and a tad pricier, antiques hunters and design aficionados will appreciate the tightly curated selection, which requires less weeding through junk heaps to find your treasure. Home décor is a strong suit – the big typography letter signs and vintage prints sold here decorate many a chic apartment.

The **Strasse des 17. Juni Flea Market**, on the edge of Tiergarten Park, has an equally upscale slant. Besides the typical mix, the specialty here is older stuff, like 19th-century porcelain, brass candlesticks, silverware and oil paintings in ornate wooden frames. Most of the tables here are manned by pro sellers, so prepare to bargain hard if it's a fantastic deal you seek.

ARKONAPLATZ FLEA MARKET

In contrast, the bustling **Boxhagener Platz Flea Market** in Friedrichshain has a chill, neighborhood feel. Some of the best deals are to be found here, as many of the vendors are residents clearing out their old clothes and clutter. If it's nostalgic 1970s East German stuff or classic records that float your boat, this is where you should explore.

When the weather isn't cooperating, make your way to **Arena Flea Market**. The indoor setup in a former train warehouse is crammed from floor to ceiling with stuff, enough to keep dedicated hunters occupied for hours. Don't expect to find much vintage clothing here, but rather lots of household items like lamps, alarm clocks and crockery, mixed in with old cameras and radios.

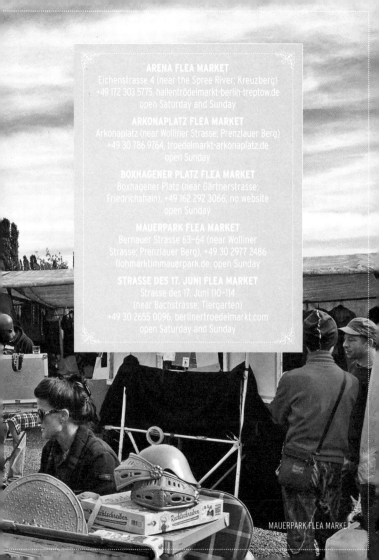

ARENA FLEA MARKET
Eichenstrasse 4 (near the Spree River; Kreuzberg)
+49 172 303 5775, hallentrödelmarkt-berlin-treptow.de
open Saturday and Sunday

ARKONAPLATZ FLEA MARKET
Arkonaplatz (near Wolliner Strasse; Prenzlauer Berg)
+49 30 786 9764, troedelmarkt-arkonaplatz.de
open Sunday

BOXHAGENER PLATZ FLEA MARKET
Boxhagener Platz (near Gärtnerstrasse;
Friedrichshain), +49 162 292 3066, no website
open Sunday

MAUERPARK FLEA MARKET
Bernauer Strasse 63–64 (near Wolliner
Strasse; Prenzlauer Berg), +49 30 2977 2486
flohmarktimmauerpark.de, open Sunday

STRASSE DES 17. JUNI FLEA MARKET
Strasse des 17. Juni 110–114
(near Bachstrasse; Tiergarten)
+49 30 2655 0096, berlinertroedelmarkt.com
open Saturday and Sunday

MAUERPARK FLEA MARKET

charlottenburg-
wilmersdorf

Unlike the dynamic neighborhoods over on the eastern side of the capital, Charlottenburg and its sibling, Wilmersdorf, have a more settled, stately and historic feel. This bourgeois area on the western side has long been where the genteel upper crust choose to live, and a cocktail or a meal will typically run a few euros more than elsewhere in Berlin. The most high-end shopping in the city is out here, along and around the grand Kurfürstendamm boulevard. The famous Kaufhaus des Westens, or KaDeWe, an enormous department store positively dripping with luxury, remains as popular today as when it opened in 1905. To experience a more low-key side of the hood, head to Savignyplatz, with its manicured flower beds and sidewalk terraces.

C/O Berlin
Café im Literaturhaus
Chelsea Farmers Club
Glass
Paper & Tea
Rogacki (off map)
Schwarzes Café

C/O BERLIN

Through different perspectives

Hardenbergstrasse 22-24 (near Joachimsthaler Strasse)
+49 30 2844 4160 / co-berlin.org / Open daily

Over the last century, photography rapidly rose to become one of the most widespread and approachable art forms. The C/O Berlin gallery brings together some of the greatest work from the world of contemporary visual media, running several concurrent exhibitions at a time showcasing both lesser-known talents as well as legendary names like Anton Corbijn, Martin Parr and Josef Koudelka. After more than a decade in Mitte, the exhibition center moved in late 2014 to its current location in the Amerika Haus, a blocky, coolly retro 1950s building that was once a West Berlin cultural center run by the American government

CAFÉ IM LITERATURHAUS

Classic coffeehouse with regular author readings

Fasanenstrasse 23 (near Kurfürstendamm)   +49 30 882 5414
literaturhaus-berlin.de / Open daily

While most of this 19th-century villa is used by a literary organization, the main floor is given over to an elegant café that's open to everyone. With gilded, scrolled stucco on the ceilings, art on the walls and an atmosphere of grandeur lurking in every corner, it's a handsome and inspiring space for a meal or a drink. I think the nicest times to come are for a fancy breakfast treat or in the late afternoon, when it's German custom to take a break for *kaffee und kuchen* (coffee and cake). In the summer, there are tables out front in the garden, while on chillier days, the choice seats in the house are in the glass-ceilinged conservatory.

CHELSEA FARMERS CLUB

Spiffy finds for fashionable men

Schlüterstrasse 50 (near Mommsenstrasse) / **+49 30 8872 7474**
chelseafarmersclub.de / **Closed Sunday**

Nobody does dapper quite as well as the Brits. From tweed jackets to cuff links, cashmere socks to riding boots, Chelsea Farmers Club has all the requisite British pieces a gentleman needs from head to toe, whether he's heading to a polo match or just out on the town. The smart range of pieces sourced from fair Britannia includes summer suits in striped seersucker, carved walking sticks, pocket squares, brogues so well made they can last a lifetime, whiskey flasks and a hat for every occasion. Plus, the self-serve gin and tonic bar ensures an even more enjoyable shopping experience.

GLASS

Daring, inventive nosh

Uhlandstrasse 195 (near Steinplatz) / **+49 30 5471 0861**
glassberlin.de / **Closed Sunday and Monday**

Glass is easily the most adventurous restaurant in Charlottenburg.
A true culinary artist, chef and owner Gal Ben-Moshe takes inspiration
from the world around him to create his five- and seven-course tasting
menus, and when he says every dish should tell a story, he really means
it. When I dined here, he popped out of the kitchen to share anecdotes
of how a walk in the park or the smell of autumn leaves influenced this
or that creation. His famed Candy Box dessert, based on a treasured
memory of a childhood picnic, is served right on a tabletop mat, scattered
with sweet delights like homemade marshmallows and chocolate
mousse frozen before your eyes with liquid nitrogen.

PAPER & TEA

The world's finest brews

Bleibtreustrasse 4 (near Kantstrasse) / **+49 30 555 798 080**
paperandtea.com / Closed Sunday

I say it's a disgrace that so many people drink awful, mass-produced tea and know nothing better. With their exceptional inventory of pure, top-quality leaves sourced from small gardens around the globe, Paper & Tea reveals the boundless potential of the multifaceted, multitalented camellia sinensis. The minimalist, Zen-like aesthetic of the shop creates a tranquil atmosphere to sip a few samples and discover the extensive range of black, green, white and oolong from China, Japan and Taiwan as well as lesser-known sources such as Nepal and Kenya. A curation of exquisite brewing accessories and handmade paper products rounds out the selection.

ROGACKI

Deluxe German deli

Wilmersdorfer Strasse 145 (at Spielhagenstrasse) / +49 30 343 8250
rogacki.de / Closed Sunday

More than any other district, Charlottenburg is where traditions persist, and Rogacki is a fine example: now managed by the grandson of the founders, the family-run deli dates back to 1928. One glass case after another hold a trove of German delicacies, such as fresh fish, smoked or pickled, every kind of wurst imaginable, pungent cheeses and hefty rye loaves. One of the biggest draws is the lunch counter at the back, which bustles with gray-haired residents feasting on everything from crispy fish fillets to roast suckling pig to oysters. I always go for a native specialty called boulette, a fist-sized fried meatball served with your choice of three different potato salads.

SCHWARZES CAFÉ

Drinks and food 'round the clock

Kantstrasse 148 (near Savignyplatz) / **+49 30 313 8038**
schwarzescafe-berlin.de / **Open daily**

There are some times in life when you just need a club sandwich, a milkshake and a tumbler of whiskey at 4am. Schwarzes Café, an area institution since 1978, has us night owls covered. They're open pretty much nonstop (save for a few hours Tuesday morning when the cleaners come), but unlike the average, super-sleazy 24-hour establishments out there, Schwarzes Café actually has style and character. It's spread over two levels of an early 1900s building, and the high, decorated ceilings and wooden furnishings lend a touch of class. From young to old, the scene is mixed and convivial, especially early on weekend mornings when the post-club breakfast crowd streams in.

park life

Where Berliners enjoy the great outdoors

GÖRLITZER PARK
Enter from Skalitzer Strasse 47 (at Görlitzer
Strasse, Kreuzberg), +49 30 902 988 024, berlin.de

HASENHEIDE
Enter from Hasenheide (at Jahnstrasse, Kreuzberg)
+49 30 902 988 024, visitberlin.de/en/spot/
hasenheide-park

PREUSSENPARK
Enter from Brandenburgische (at Konstanzer
Strasse, Charlottenburg-Wilmersdorf)
+49 30 902 916 620, berlin.de

TEMPELHOFER FELD
Enter from Herrfurthstrasse (at Oderstrasse,
Neukölln), +49 30 700 906 859
gruen-berlin.de/tempelhofer-feld

TIERGARTEN PARK
Strasse des 17. Juni (at Grosser Stern, Tiergarten)
+49 30 901 833 101, visitberlin.de/en/spot/tiergarten

GÖRLITZER PARK

It can get pretty gray up here in the north of Europe, so whenever the sun makes an appearance, everyone relishes the opportunity to spend time in the parks. Whether for picnicking, jogging or flopping out on a blanket with some friends, Berlin's green plots are some of the best places to experience local life.

Every park has its own personality, and the most grandiose one by far is **Tempelhofer Feld**. The former Tempelhof Airport was put out of operation in 2008 and its grounds opened to the public shortly after. The runways are still intact and attract plenty of cyclists, runners and even kiteboarders. This is one of the most beloved picnic destinations in the city, and the unbroken expanse of green space offers a wonderful feeling of openness.

Those of us living in Neukölln sure are lucky – directly adjacent to Tempelhofer Feld is **Hasenheide**. With both open fields and forested parts towering with lovely oak trees, Hasenheide has a mix of terrains to suit every taste, plus a petting zoo for kids. Funnily enough, the area always draws slackliners who practice on ropes strung up between trees.

In the neighboring district of Kreuzberg, the place where everyone hangs out is **Görlitzer Park**. It's rather on the scruffy side, but what it lacks in landscaping it makes up for in liveliness. Near the northern end is a big bowl-shaped recess in the grass where much of the action happens. Be it drum circles, gaggles of punks swigging beer or Turkish families barbecuing kebabs, Görlitzer Park is the place to witness a colorful slice of neighborhood life.

In contrast, **Tiergarten Park** is a bit of pastoral peace in the heart of town, wound through with streams and ponds. Once the private hunting grounds of the Prussian royals, today's Tiergarten Park is the city's second-largest public garden (after Tempelhofer Feld). It's mostly wooded, making it good for shaded jogging, and the trees divide the park up into little pockets, with picnics and even gay cruising finding their private corners.

The most surprising experience is **Preussenpark** in Wilmersdorf. On weekends, scores of Thai women cook and sell authentic specialties right there on the grass, from noodle soups and spicy papaya salad to fried whole fish and even shaved ice desserts. You can even get a Thai massage right there on your picnic blanket.

TEMPELHOFER FELD